A Brother's Love

DeAndré Holmes

India | USA | UK

Copyright © DeAndré Holmes
All Rights Reserved.

This book has been self-published with all reasonable efforts taken to make the material error-free by the author. No part of this book shall be used, reproduced in any manner whatsoever without written permission from the author, except in the case of brief quotations embodied in critical articles and reviews.

The Author of this book is solely responsible and liable for its content including but not limited to the views, representations, descriptions, statements, information, opinions, and references ["Content"]. The Content of this book shall not constitute or be construed or deemed to reflect the opinion or expression of the Publisher or Editor. Neither the Publisher nor Editor endorse or approve the Content of this book or guarantee the reliability, accuracy, or completeness of the Content published herein and do not make any representations or warranties of any kind, express or implied, including but not limited to the implied warranties of merchantability, fitness for a particular purpose.

The Publisher and Editor shall not be liable whatsoever...

Made with ❤ on the BookLeaf Publishing Platform
www.bookleafpub.in
www.bookleafpub.com

Dedication

Shout out to God! I found me and I found Peace!
#DreInTheA

Preface

This book is simply, OBEDIENCE. God has been working in and through me to make me more like His Son, Jesus, each and every day. Poetry is one of the ways I Glorify my Father and express my Love for Who and What He Is. His Word is Alive and Active, which is why it's written on the Tablet of My Heart and flows through my poetry. This book is meant to spread The Good News of our Sovereign Lord. Every poem is an illustration of, "I Am That I Am."

Acknowledgements

Lord God, I Thank You for The Ultimate Sacrifice of Your One and Only Begotten Son. For the sake of mankind, You sent Your Son into the world to be The Atonement of our sins. We don't deserve Your Love, Grace nor Mercy, but I Thank You for Them. I Thank You for providing us with a way to our Salvation. I Thank You for being the same today, tomorrow and forever. There's no one above You, Lord. You're The First and The Last. All Praise, Glory and Honor belong to You.

To my Lord and Savior, Jesus Christ, I Love You more than Life Itself. Thank You for being Born into sin, and Living a Perfect Life, despite all You Endured. Thank You for being The Way, The Truth and The Life. Mankind has access to Eternal Life because of Your Selflessness. Many are Invited, but only a Few are Chosen. Thank You for setting me Apart.

Thank You, Holy Spirit, Advocate, Comforter for Interceding on my behalf. Thank You for Convicting me and keeping me Honest. Continue to bring Scripture to my remembrance, and Lead me in the way I should go. Guide every thought I think, every word I speak and all the actions I take. See to it that I Live in Alignment with my Father's Will, according to His Plan and Purpose for me.

1. I Am Somebody

My Brother,
A nation has been built upon your very back.
My brother, pity the fool if you think you'll get credit for any of that.

My brother, pull yourself up by your boot straps even though you're traveling barefoot.
My brother, watch out for the worldly traps along the way; they'll surely get you hooked.

My brother, turn the other cheek and keep fighting the good fight.
My brother, this is a never ending war. Be prepared to fight all day and night.

My brother, when you make it out don't forget to reach back for another.
My brother, be sure to have a strong base while reaching back, the crabs in the barrel would love to add another.

My brother, head up, shoulders back, carry yourself with integrity and dignity.
My brother, satan masquerades around like an Angel of Light; watch out for your frenemies.

My brother, my brother, everyone isn't of the dark.
My brother, my brother you are The Light, and I'm here to give you a spark.

My brother, God is in you, so who cares who's against you.
My brother, you'll be Raised Up by His Righteous Right Hand, and He'll make them all your footstool.

My brother, good brother, carry on and Count It All Joy.
Good brother, good brother Life's a game, so cherish and play it as if you're a child with its favorite toy.

2. Soulful

Strip me of this flesh and get to know the real me.
Only the Son of Man will know what you'll truly see.
It'll be nothing you can think of and far more than you can imagine.
Few may say I'm skinny, but God be my witness, I'm far from famine.
I Eat of The Lord's Word and Drink of His Spirit too.
I'm clothed in His Love and Grace, like the Autumn grass masked in the morning dew.
I'm forever Evolving, my Mind is made New.
My Spirit is Infinite, I've Lived a Lifetime or two.
How long til I remember, what I've come here to do.
Remembrance is my goal, I hope the same for you too.
I'm Purpose driven to my Core. I've put down the worldly views.
I Seek only what God has for me, which landed me on the list of the enemy's to do.
I worry not because God is for me, so it doesn't matter what forms against me.
I've put on The Full Armor of God,

I shall not contemplate defeat.

3. Righteousness

Deeply rooted in Faith, for sin I've lost all taste.
Very Narrow The Gate, all through the wide will go to waste.

With The Key of Obedience, all doors will be unlocked.
In the midst of adversity, Seek God so Blessings aren't blocked.

Love thy neighbor dearly, for our Father has Commanded.
He IS our Savior, Son of Man Set The Standard.

Rest in His Love, for there's no better place.
Dwell in His Presence, may our sins be met with Grace.

Heaven is on Earth, for I know that to be True.
Live through The Spirit, so you'll know like I do.

The Heart will be tested, make Pure of your Intentions.

You're here to be a Vessel, for that the enemy will Seek vengeance.

4. New Creation

I've taken The Water, iniquity was laid to rest in The Liquid Grave.
My slate has been Washed Clean, Forgiven I've been for all the mistakes I've made.
Iridescent is The One I stand before, Born Again and made New.
I've chosen to Surrender; how good it feels to be one of The Few.
Lead me to my Purpose Lord; help me exalt Your Holy Kingdom.
I'm Your Sheep, Shepherd and Disciple; Thank You for giving me my Freedom.
Free from the anguish of the world; at Your Right Hand is where I'm seated.
Pour into my New Wine Skin; the former was worn, dry and depleted.
I come forth willing and ready to Serve; use me as You See Fit.
This Life was never meant for my gain; pleasing You is how I'll make the most of it.

I've chosen to only die once; from a single womb was I Born twice.
Lord, I Rest in Your Comfort; for every battle of mine shall You fight.
Make me more like Your Son Jesus; Faithful, Honorable and Blameless.
Faithfulness is a Promise I vow to keep; I shall not depart from this Earth nameless.
You knew me before my Mother and Father; they done with me the best that they could.
Back to You I've come running; as a child trained up The Right Way should.

5. The Way, The Truth, The Life

Come as you are and draw closer to your Creator.
He's The Source of Eternal Life, there is no one greater.
Through the Almighty Jesus Christ, is the Way to The Father.
He Loves Saints and sinners, Seek Him to get your Life in order.
What's a Life without Faith?
Picture the Braves without their ace.
That would be your Life story.
Worrisome and wrapped in purgatory.
So come one, come all.
He doesn't promise you won't fall.
But for your good will it be.
If you let The Holy Spirit take the lead.
Be sure not to straddle the fence.
Turning back leads to Recompense.
Reluctant servants are beaten with Many Stripes.
Devote your Mind, Body and Soul to Jesus Christ.

Either you're Living of The Spirit or perishing of the body.
Only one is of God, be sure to choose wisely.
Faith is Believing in The Unseen. Like chasing after your wildest dream.
Or boarding an aircraft, with a pilot you've never seen.
Walk with God and discover your Ministry.
The Pulpit may not be your scenery.
Be sure to boast about The Lord and spread all of The Good News.
With the Seat comes The Cup.
Are you fit to walk in His Shoes?

6. Sonship

Thank you, Lord, for the renewing of my Mind, Heart and Soul.
Obedient is Your Son, I vow to do as I'm told.
I've forgotten the former things, all of The New I do Perceive.
Thank you, for opening my eyes this morning, Blessing me with another opportunity to Breathe.

For all things work together for the good of those who Love You.
I've been Called according to Your Purpose, reveal to me Thy Will to do.
All of my Trust is in You, I can't fathom Worshipping another.
The proof is in The Text, you knew me before I entered The Womb of my Mother.

Now to You who is able to do Immeasurably more than all we can Ask or Imagine.

I Count It All Joy because Your Power at work within me isn't passive.
I will make known to the world Who is at The Head of my Life.
Lord, spreading The Good News is an Honor; for me You Paid The Ultimate Price.

7. At His Feet

The Righteous will Inherit The Land.
The wicked will not stand a chance.
Trust that their Harvest will be short Lived.
Joy comes in the morning, so wipe your tears.
You've endured enough, now rise to your feet.
In times of famine, trust you'll have meat.
He'll provide for your every need.
Leave to the wicked all envy and greed.
Blessed are the children who Seek Thee.
Mocked are the ones that incite foolery.
So draw near and lay at The Feet of our Lord Jesus.
He has made room for all of His Believers.

8. I Found Me and I Found Peace

I discovered a lot sitting in Solitude.
Allow me to Inspire you.
Not by the things that I've obtained, but by The Wisdom in my brain.
Not by the waves in my hair, nor the garments on my back.
But by the way I deny the flesh, by removing lust and lack.
Not by the car that I drive, nor the white of my smile,
But by The Brightness of The Light, Shining through my inner child.
Not by The Gifts that I bear.
If I could I would spare,
But how I make space for you to be Authentic and True.
I dare you not to care what any one thinks.
To be quite honest and frank, they'll be gone in a blink.
So put your trust in The Man,
Who giveth and taketh without lifting a hand.
And He'll clearly direct your Path,

according to His Purpose and Plan.

9. Haughty Man

What good is a man that gains the world but loses his Soul?
What good is a man who Seeks God but disobeys what he's told?
What good is a man who cherishes his Mother but despises his Father?
Good man you can Repent, but without change, why even bother?
What good is a man who works hard but neglects his kids.
What good is a man who tells The Truth, but never what he did.
What good is a man who Worships, but dances with the devil?
Good man you're digging your own grave. Put down that shovel.
Nevertheless, when you call God, He picks up the phone.
It's such a mess, when God calls you,
You're never home.

10. Be Still and Know That I Am God

In order to hear God's Word, you may have to be all alone.
By The Life you're Living, you wouldn't be allowed to cast The First Stone.
So walk away from the things, that no longer serve you.
Sit Still and wait on The Lord, Patience is a Virtue.

God gave His Only Son for The Good of mankind.
How long will it take the entire world to Worship The Divine.
Where two or three gather in His Name He will be with them.
He doesn't need the entire world just a few that Believe in Him.

Be Faithful to The Lord and He'll provide for your every need.
It may not look like what you want, but it's for your greater good, so take heed.

Blessed are The Poor in Spirit, The Peacemakers, The Pure in Heart.
Blessed are The Meek, The Merciful, and Those Mourning in the dark.

Now tell all that'll listen how Good God Is.
I know you heard about The Five Loaves of Bread and The Two Fish.
Or what about the time He turned Water into Wine?
I can assure you that's not something you heard through the grapevine.

Carve out some time for The Lord daily and He'll Right your Path.
You plus The Lord is Unstoppable, now that's some easy math.

Bank with The Lord, be frank with The Lord, ask Him to guide you to and from.
Eat with The Lord, sleep with The Lord, It'll be the best thing you've ever done.

11. God's Will

If you knew how it would work out, there would be no point in Faith.
If you knew how it would work out, would you be in the same place?
If you knew how it would work out, there would be no point in God.
If you knew how it would work out, would you go against all odds?

You don't know how it'll work out, so don't deprive yourself by Walking By Sight.
You don't know how it'll work out, so Live Life to fullest and remove all of your maybe and I mights.
You don't know how it'll work out, so take risk and take chances.
You don't know how it'll work out, but may your chances bring you advancement.

God knows how it'll work out, so why wouldn't you want Him in your Life?

God knows how it'll work out, He'll lighten your load and remove the strife.
God knows how it'll work out, ask Him to order your steps in His Word.
God has it all worked out, that's why he removed you from the herd.

12. Love, Grace and Mercy

Without Your Mercy Lord, I'd be in a world of trouble.
Despite my sins and shortcomings, You've Raised me up and Blessed me with double.
O' Lord tell me what I've done to deserve such Grace.
I'm Grateful You chose me, so each and every day I will Seek Your Face.

Lord, I know You're with me everywhere that I go.
No weapon formed against me shall Prosper, for that I know.
You granted me The Power to Condemn the enemy.
Lord, I Love You with All My Heart, I know You Dwell within me.

You said to bring all of my Tithes into Your Storehouse of Improvement.
Lord, have Your Way in my Life,
All I need to do is Sit Still.
There's worry in movement.

Lord, it's written in The Text that if I ask not and I have not.
I ask that you allow me to Dwell in Your Secret Place, and to never lose my spot.

13. Heart Posture

Like snow in the Summer or rain in Harvest, honor is not fitting for a fool.
The Lord is my Shepherd, I shall not want. He has Sharpened and Equipped me with Every Tool.
In the midst of adversity, I stand firm in Certainty. I will not allow doubt nor fear to creep in.
He makes me lie down in Green Pastures and leads me by Still Waters; I will not wallow with the pigs in pin.
Son of Man is my Savior, I mimic His Behavior. He is The Beginning and The End.
Lord, you are my Friend, remove from me all sin. He won't allow me to break, but I will bend.

14. Surrender

How long will you wait until you take matters into your own hands?
It's funny that you thought your Life would go according to your own plans.
God is at Helm, He needs no help from mere mortals.
His Strength is Sufficient in your weakness, He'll relieve you of all your struggle.
Relinquish control and fix your eyes on your Lord and Savior.
You don't have a Rod nor a Staff; be sure to thank The Lord for His Favor.
With knowledge comes Understanding, If you know better, please do better.
Because The Wrath of The Almighty will have you pleading like a Love letter.

15. Jehovah Jireh

As I look back on my Life, I've never gone a day begging Bread.
The Lord has always provided, I've never gone a night without a place to lay my Head.
I put all of my Trust and Faith in The One Who knows The End from The Beginning.
Despite me being born into sin, His Living Water has quenched my thirst of sinning.

I thank The Lord for Him, His Son and The Holy Spirit.
I've been Delivered and filled with Confidence through His Words of endearment.

If I can be frank, Life is an open book test.
But my name isn't Frank, open your Bible and be Blessed.
Be sure to take it a step further, obtaining His Knowledge isn't enough.
It's imperative to Live out His Word, the devil will call your bluff.

16. Jehovah Nissi

Think about what you're thinking about, so you're in the right mindset.
The Lord is my Shepherd, I shall not want, so therefore I know I'm Blessed.
He may not come when I want Him to, but He's never a second too late.
Like the boys in Fiery Furnace, I'll never denounce my Faith.
I've felt The Lord's Presence; it's unlike anything of the world.
He's so clever with His Messages; He spoke to me through a pretty girl.
I'm Anointed and I know it; with Power comes many Lessons.
Let your Light Shine before men and Glorify your Father Who's in Heaven.

17. Jehovah Shalom

You want Peace?
Prepare for war.
It's never ending like stuffing air inside a jar.
Both internal and external is where your battles will take place.
Whether seen or unseen, they both take up space.
What is space?
Space can be where your Peace lies.
War can be the very thing that results in your demise.
Peace is achieved, worked for and earned.
You have to look inward and face the darkness.
You'll find Peace on the other side of the burn.

18. Jehovah Rapha

To The One who is above all else.
Who knows of every pain I've felt.
To The One who overcame the entire world.
Who knew before my Mother that I'd be a boy and not a girl.
To The One who became flesh and Lived a Perfect Life.
Who knew of The Joy coming through His enduring of strife.
To The One who made Disciples of many men.
Who knew that His Ministering would lead to less sin.
To The One who was denied, shamed and discouraged.
Who knew He was sent to bear all of my burdens.
To The One who put others before Himself.
Who knew that Love would Conquer all else.
To The One who told me how to Love my neighbor.
Who knew that His Blood being shed would be my Savior.
To The One who gives and seldom takes.
Who knows my Faith determines my Fate.
To The One who created everything known to mankind.

Who knows how many times He'd open my eyes to see the Sun Shine.
To The One who goes by Jesus Christ.
Who knew I'd Love Him more than my own Life.
Truly, how close are you to our Creator?
I suggest you get to know Him sooner rather than later.

19. Grace

One thing I know is you just can't beat God's Giving.
You'll find yourself outside of God's Will if you keep on sinning.
Your Walk with God will require you to change your playmates and your playground.
By the thoughts you think and the actions you take, so will you be bound.
Whatever you bind on Earth will be bound in Heaven, and whatever you loose on Earth will be loosed in Heaven.

How good is your Soil, is The Word landing on 30, 60 or 100?
Don't allow the devil to oppose The Lord's Word and strip from you your Birthright of Abundance.
Before He made me a New Creation, I'll tell you it felt good to feed the flesh.
Not knowing my lustful thoughts and acts would land me in a pile of mess.

As I sat all alone, I looked around to find no one to blame.
You couldn't tell I was raised in The Church by my actions, it was such a shame.
Yes, I Prayed, I acknowledge God,
But there wasn't an intimate relationship.
Yet, He still Blessed me, and always Protected me.
Being one of His comes with many benefits.

My Blessings aren't for my personal gain, but for The Uplifting of His Kingdom.
He knew He could use me to lead others to their God Given Freedom.
I was a shy kid, very reserved, for that I know These Words aren't mine.
The Lord is Working in me and through me, it's a command and a duty to Let My Light So Shine.

20. Salvation

Be Still and know that I Am God.
Fix your eyes on Me, those worldly facets are all a facade.
I'm offering you Eternal Life, not a trend nor a gimmick.
There are a lot of mortals claiming My Power, although, I can't be mimicked.

Press forward with Unwavering Faith, My Word will never return to Me Void.
Why try to do Life on your own? I'm The Dealer Who Dealt you The Cards.
Build your Faith on My Wisdom, I got all you'll ever need.
I know The End from The Beginning. How much longer until My Child Believes?

I created everything known to mankind, and made man in My Image and Likeness.
I've pPaced My Spirit inside you, the dark has no chance against My Brightness.

I'm The First and The Last, who can contend with My Mighty Wrath?
I'm the same today, tomorrow and forever, My Ways lead The Narrow Path.

Pick up your Cross and deny your flesh daily.
My Ways are consistent, I could never be shady.
My Grace Is Sufficient, I'm not asking you to be perfect.
I require your Obedience, I can guarantee you it'll be worth it.

Make Me your Fortress, your Cornerstone, your Refuge, your Rock.
Doors will be opened unto you, if you dare to Ask, Seek and Knock.

Don't envy the ways of the wicked.
It's True, looks can be deceiving.
Before long their riches will be gone,
and those perishing Souls will be begging and pleading.

I'm The Way to your Salvation, it's imperative you make me your Stronghold.
All alone you are small and timid, for My Use you'll become Big and Bold.
I've told you I'm a Jealous God; never deny Me of My Praise.

I always knew you'd come Home, and put an end to your worldly ways.

21. Blessings

Delight yourself in The Lord
and He will give you the Desires of your Heart.
Fret not because of evildoers,
allow God to do His Part.

22. Life or Death

Living in flow
allows one to let go.
Living in sin
leads to an early end.

23. Patience

Never rush,
what's meant will come.
Sit Still,
what's yours is already Done.

24. Love Your Neighbor as Yourself

Love all,
for everyone is equal.
Fear not,
Jesus Lived The Prequel.

25. It's Better to Give Than Receive

Lend a hand when you can,
make the most of your days.
Son of Man Rules The Land,
evil has no place.

26. Freedom

Arise!
Shine!
Live a Risen Life.
Brag!
Boast!
God removed all strife.

27. I Know Who and Who's I Am

Here I sit, with intentions to appease.
Knowing not what to say, I'm a man of many but less words.
Always under control and never absurd.
I know who I am, so who I'm not I'll never be.
I speak what I Seek and I Seek to become who God placed me on This Earth to be,
Purposefully!

28. Peace

I lie here, mind empty but full of space and time.
I have zero interests but yearn for excitement, almost like a first grader waiting on play time.
No matter where I go nor who I meet, I'm always at Peace.
I'm the best version of myself because I simply, Seek Thee and Be.

29. Contentment

Thinking I need more while content with knowing others have less.
Stuck between chasing feats and achievements and sitting Still and getting some Rest.
I know not where I'm going, but at Peace with wherever I'll be.
It's for certain that I'm Truly Blessed because He Resides in me.

30. Creator's Creation

In a hammock, amongst Nature where True Freedom lies.
No sense of time besides the time of year because it appears that all of the leaves have died.
That I believe not because energy is Eternal and Infinite like Source.
I find Peace in knowing myself and the animals are all subjective to Mother Nature taking Its Course.

31. Truth

The world can be controlled by The Truth.
The Truth can stand alone.

The Truth has a ring to it, even a sting to it.
So much so that it'll leave one all on their own.

The Truth has a gleam to it, even a bling to it.
So much so that it'll wipe the dirty clean.

The Truth is Righteous and Honorable,
it needs no additional facts.
So Righteous and So Honorable,
The Truth Is Just That.

32. Who Are You

Who are you?
Are you the flesh, your thoughts, or emotions?
Are you those eyes, that smile, or your inner child?
Are you what you wear, what you drive, or where you Live?
Are you who they say you are, your past or who God has called you to be?
Hey, I'm asking the questions here, so don't ask me.

33. Heart's Desires

You call yourself a dreamer, huh?
How vivid are these dreams?
Are they average?
Are they for self?
Do they require your Spiritual Team?
Do they shock you?
Do they scare you?
Are they minuscule?
Are they darest?
I know one thing for fact.
Only you can answer that.

How deep are you going into depth?
Are these dreams demanding any help?
Unto whom shall you call?
There's Only One Who won't let you fall.
Young fellow, here's a piece of advice.
Call unto no one other than Jesus Christ.

34. The Lord's House

Come by here, my Lord, come by here.
Protect me with Your Sword, remove from me any fear.
I know my many Blessings are stored, I'll enter into Your House and Cheer.
I'll make a Joyful Noise, O' Lord, lend me an ear.
Come by here, my Lord, come by here.

35. Love

Love
There's a million words to describe it.
Yet, it's unexplainable.
Many of us lack it.
But rest assured it's attainable.

36. Pink Ribbon

To the ones we've lost and to the ones that Survived and are Thriving.
May God grant you Peace to experience days of Living and not Surviving.
Every year holds another test.
I Decree and Declare your days will be Blessed.
It matters not what the results say.
For our Father has The Final Ye or Ne.
May He grant you Rest and not just sleep.
There's nothing too big for Him to defeat.
So walk about Earth with your Head High.
Trust that the doubt and fear are all lies.
Whether you have one, two or none,
For you, God sent His Only Son.
This world is nothing without you.
I assure all 365 are about you.
For we'll never forget the ones we've lost and cherish the ones that Survive.
May every year of a Clean Bill of Health not come to you as a Surprise.

37. Family

Family is meant to have fun with, bond with, maybe even sit by a pond with.
Family is meant to share Pure Love, a hug, be each other's dose of drugs.
Family is everything, as precious as a wedding ring.
Family should make your Heart sing, can't be replace with anything.
Family is Heaven Sent, a place of comfort and time spent.
Family is forever, Family is a Treasure.
Whether on Earth or in Heaven, Family is a Blessing.

38. Light

Beauty
Is the way curves and shapes,
Bend and brake,
As The Light Shines upon
The.

39. Steadfast

On your journey through Life,
You'll see and learn a lot.
Be sure to not get caught
Not knowing something twice.

Here's a piece of advice that you can take with you forever.
Behind those mountains are more mountains,
It doesn't get easier, You just get better.

www.ingramcontent.com/pod-product-compliance
Lightning Source LLC
Chambersburg PA
CBHW060354050426
42449CB00011B/2988